YPS

Think about it...
Precious Planet

Harry Cory Wright

W

FRANKLIN WATTS
LONDON • SYDNEY

Look at the sky.

What can you see?

What would it be like
to live in this valley?

Why is water important?

How do you think this feather got here?

What might the farmer grow in this field?

Where do these things come from?

How many different materials can you see?

What do you think you
might find in this pond?

How could some of these things be recycled?

How does this picture make you feel? What kind of day was it?

How does this picture make you feel?
Is it a good feeling?

Look at this flower.
What does its shape remind you of?

Are these flowers big or small?
What might they feel like?

What would it be like to be in this city?

What would it be like to play here?

What might you see in the city at night?

What would it feel like to walk along this beach?

If you could paint
a picture of a place,
where would it be?

Precious Planet

What do we think of the world around us? What are the questions that help us to engage with, and understand, our environment? The pictures in this book aim to inspire the viewer to think about our planet, from its beauty to its fragility. The questions that accompany the pictures try to provide a sense of protection and belonging while stimulating imagination.

A framework for exploration

'What's going on in this picture?' is a question that is asked by children and adults alike whenever presented with a photograph. Usually the answer is in the caption. But what if we ask questions rather than provide answers? What if there is no right answer? The photographs in this book are intended to be starting points for children to explore ideas. Remember, there are no rules here, let alone any right answers – children can take a simple idea and run with it as far as they wish.

The teacher or parent should use his or her judgement to decide the appropriate depth of discussion according to the abilities of the child. Some children may describe only what they see in the picture in clear sentences. Other children should be able to extend the themes and offer in depth explanations and opinions. Ideas for expanding each theme are listed below in 'Talk about', but you may also ask some general questions on the theme of a precious planet such as: What do you feel about this scene? Why should we respect our planet?

Look at the sky. What can you see? (pages 2–3)
This picture was taken on a hot day. But later the clouds thickened and a thunderstorm broke out.
Talk about: • what clouds are • why the sky looks blue • different types of cloud • space • changing weather • what shapes you can see in the clouds.

What would it be like to live in this valley? (pages 4–5)
This is Borrowdale in the Lake District. It is early spring and although the fields are green, the trees are yet to show their leaves. Early morning sun gives an awakening feel. Find out how many children have visited the area. Ask them to share their experiences.
Talk about: • which season it is – how can they tell • the field shapes • what animals might be on the hills • what animals might be in the river • what buildings might be in the village.

Why is water important? (page 6)
Water is vital and no one can live without it. Encourage the children to think about all the things we need water for, such as drinking, washing, growing plants etc.
Talk about: • the water cycle in simple terms • floods • droughts • the importance of wells in developing countries • pollution of water – effects on wildlife and humans.

How do you think this feather got here? (page 7)
Encourage the children to think about what sort of bird this feather has come from. What does a feather feel like?
Talk about: • why birds have feathers • how much a feather might weigh • how some birds can fly noiselessly, e.g. owl, and why this helps it hunt for prey.

What might the farmer grow in this field? (pages 8–9)
This field has just been sown with leeks. The farmer grows leeks here every year, as did his father. It is a lovely early spring day and the farmer is waiting for the rain.
Talk about: • other crops that farmers sow • why do they grow crops? • what plants do the children grow at home? • what plants have they spotted in communal places such as parks? • what do crops need to grow? • different soils and growing environments • how plants develop – roots followed by shoots.

Where do these things come from? How many different materials can you see?
(pages 10–11)

Here is a huge array of equipment for every kind of vacuum cleaner.

Talk about: • why we need to clean up after ourselves • recycling parts from old pieces of equipment • how plastic is made /recycled and re-used.

What do you think you might find in this pond?
(pages 12–13)

This is my son Joe doing what he loves, which is to look for animals of all kinds in watery places. There are springs here that come out of the chalk. All manner of wildlife thrive around these willow trees and on a warm spring day the place teams with life.

Talk about: • what the area is like • have they ever played in a place like this? • the wildlife in the pond and woods • caring for environments such as this • respecting wildlife • staying safe around water.

How could some of these things be recycled? (pages 14–15)

This is inside a skip at a recycling centre. I spent a long time looking over such a wide variety of printed material. It was full of all manner of things to look at. All paper comes from trees and each is printed for a different purpose with a different message.

Talk about: • where do the children think this paper has come from? • why do they think it is bad to be wasteful with paper? • how paper is made (simple explanation) • what we use paper for • different types of paper and card • problems of litter • recycling paper and card.

How does this picture make you feel? What kind of day was it? (pages 16–17)

This photograph was taken from a boat in the Atlantic. It was a glorious day and we were pushing along gently sending out this wake from the boat. There is not much in the picture but I am intrigued by how uplifting it is; simple things make it

so – the sunshine, the light on the water and the sense of movement. The horizon at an altered angle gives it a different aspect.

Talk about: • how many children have been sailing at sea and what was it like? • tides • people who work at sea • animals in the sea • pollution of the sea.

How does this picture make you feel? Is it a good

feeling? (pages 18–19)

This is the Medway which runs into the River Thames. It was very foggy and the power cables above were fizzing like mad. When the fog cleared it revealed a huge power station. Notice how all the human things are wonky, as if the natural forces (time and tide) are trying to level it all. Point out that this area is tidal and that the picture has been taken at low tide. Invite the children to think of good words to describe the picture, e.g. eerie, gloomy, misty. Make a list of the words for free-writing.

Talk about: • what the crane may be used for • what the area may look like at high tide • the things humans have put in the area and why.

Look at this flower. What does its shape remind you of? Are these flowers big or small? What might they feel like?
(pages 20–21)

Encourage the children to talk about flowers they know. If possible provide flowers to handle. What do they feel like? Do they have a scent?

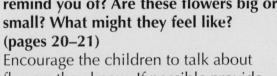

Talk about: • the shape of the petals in the pictures • what they think the flowers feel like • how flowers are cared for once they have been cut • what happens to flowers as they die.

What would it be like to be in this city? (pages 22–23)

This is a view from Waterloo Bridge in London. In spite of the rather calm feel to the picture it is full of things going on; the river flowing, the clouds above moving from left to right, the sun rising, and of course all the buildings and what goes on in and around them.

Talk about: • what this place might have looked like 100, 500 and 1,000 years ago • what it might look like in a 100 years time.

What would it be like to play here? (pages 24–25)

This is a play area in the woods in a campsite on the edge of Exmoor. It is summer time and there is a rope swing. Children play all sorts of games throughout the day here. Ask the children which season they think it is and why.

Talk about: • what games could be played here • what sounds might be heard • who the children would most like to play with in a place like this.

What might you see in the city at night? (page 26)

This is in Bristol in a very vibrant and independent part of the town. It is full of urban activity but in spite of that the trees are growing well, and there is a very healthy buddleia behind the panel, which would attract insects, including butterflies and bees. Ask the children to point out any vegetation they can see.

Talk about: • the animals you might find in a town • the plants you might see in a town • animals that might only come out when there are fewer people about, e.g. urban foxes • pollution problems in a town • what animals, such as rats and mice, might feed off in a town.

What would it feel like to walk along this beach? (page 27)

This person is a friend of mine, lost in thought on a beach in Norfolk.

Talk about: • visiting the seaside and what it feels like • what does it feel like to run on a beach in bare feet? • why the figure in the picture looks so small • scale • the weather.

If you could paint a picture of a place, where would it be? (pages 28–29)

This man is painting a hawthorn bush beside a saltmarsh in eastern England. He paints wildlife and landscape and loves the details that such a bush can provide – its shape and colour, how it has been worn and battered by the wind on a stormy day in winter, and how it can sit so beautifully in a landscape on a still spring morning. Encourage the children to deduce facts from the picture, such as how they can tell it is not windy? (The smoke is rising straight up from the chimney.) What is the most beautiful place the children have seen?

Talk about: • why people like to paint scenes such as this • the things the man would need to paint the picture • how long it would take to paint • why artists might take photos of scenes they want to paint.

First published in 2009
by Franklin Watts

Copyright © Harry Cory Wright 2009

Franklin Watts
338 Euston Road
London NW1 3BH

Franklin Watts Australia
Level 17/207 Kent Street
Sydney, NSW 2000

All rights reserved.

Series editor: Sarah Peutrill
Art director: Jonathan Hair
Consultant: Sue Graves

Dewey number: 333.7

ISBN 978 0 7496 8852 3

Printed in China

Franklin Watts is a division of Hachette Children's Books, an Hachette UK company.

www.hachette.co.uk